THERE'S
POWER
IN YOUR
"I AM"

I AM. YOU ARE. PERFECTLY IMPERFECT LLC.

Written by Kerese Millen & Kristle Millen

xulon
PRESS

Dedication

We dedicate this book to our late Grandparents, John and Odessa Millen Sr., and R.C and Mae Pearl Rogers. You four were very prominent in our lives.

We miss you guys so much. We thank you for the love and all of the times you guys kept us for the summer. Thank you, Granddaddy Millen, for getting us a baby boombox for our first car when the radio went out. We still laugh at that today. Thank you, Granddaddy Rogers, for keeping us laughing by squeezing the funny bone on our knees; we can still feel it like it was yesterday.

Thank you, Grandma Millen and Grandma Rogers, for demonstrating the strength of a woman to keep on going even when you're tired.

We can't wait to see you again.

Your Twin babies,

Kristle & Kerese

Table of Contents

Dedication v

Preface ix

The Beginning of Your "I Am" 11
(Reflect on who you are)

There's Power In your "I AM" 13
(Reflect on who you are)

There's Power In Your "I Am" 15
(Body of Thoughts)

Scripture 97
(Jerimiah 29:11)

There's Power In Your "I AM" 99
(I Am Kerese Millen)

There's Power In Your "I Am" 101
(I Am Kristle Millen)

The Beginning of Your "I Am" 105
(Reflect on who you are)

Acknowledgments 107
About the Authors 111
Connect with Kerese & Kristle Millen 113

Preface

THE REASON WHY

We have the power to change the definition that we would use to define ourselves. Why do we permit another individual to define who we are—to embed in our heads who we will become, what we will stand for? Even as children we are taught, "Whatever you put your mind to, you can do it". But the issue is that we lose that thought as we get older, going through the rejections of life. We begin to believe and ponder on the negative and not on the better outcome that's to come after the "No". Yes, we are human and we want things to go our way at all times, and when they don't we tend to pout, give up, get depressed and become stagnant.

Working with children and adults on a daily basis and studying the development of individuals and ourselves, we found out that we had the power ourselves this whole time. The two words "*I AM*" are two powerful words that can mend you, guide you, elevate you, and at the same time break you, mislead you, and demote you. The word "I" is defined as a *reference to yourself.* "**Am**" is defined as **To Be. You control your "I AM". You control who you are, who you will become, what you stand for. All it takes is taking the first steps of saying the two words, "I AM".**

This body of thoughts is a guide to help you to take control back of your "**I AM**". It starts with your "**I AM**". Who are you? What do you want to accomplish? What business do you want? What is your life's purpose? The way that we had to find out who we were was by speaking our "**I Am**". May this body of thoughts impel you to speak "**I AM**" on your daily peregrination (journey) that we call life. Remember you are the superintendent of your "**I AM**"—not the world and the people of this world. May your "**I AM** be greater than your "I WAS"!

THERE'S POWER IN YOUR "I AM"
I AM. YOU ARE. PERFECTLY IMPERFECT LLC.

The Beginning Of A New You

SPEAK YOUR "I AM"

As we go through life, we encounter different circumstances that changes the way we think of ourselves. We beat ourselves up with regrets from the choices that we have made in our lives.

We question ourselves asking, "Why? Why am I going through this? Why me? Why this? Why that?"

But have you ever thought what you are going through is happening to make you stronger?

God has been there right by your side, through the good and the bad; he's never left you even when you felt alone.

John 14: 1-4

"Do not let your hearts be troubled. Trust in God, trust also in me. In my Father's house are many rooms; If it were not so, I would have told you. I am going there to prepare a place for you. And if I go and prepare a place for you, I will come back and take you to be with me that you also may be where I am. You know the way to the place where I am going." Right now at this very moment, how would you describe your "I AM"?

I AM...

_____

_____

_____

_____

_____

_____

The Holy Bible, new international version. (1984). Grand Rapids: Zondervan Publishing House.

There's Power In Your "I Am"
I AM. YOU ARE. PERFECTLY IMPERFECT LLC.

I Am Perfectly Imperfect

DEFINITION: PERFECTLY- Entirely without flaws.

Every human being is perfect because we are a creation of God.

IMPERFECT- Flawed.

Romans 3:3-24

" *F*or we all have sinned and fall short of the glory of God, and are justified freely by his grace through the redemption that came by Christ Jesus."

Being perfectly imperfect is accepting and loving yourself passed your insecurities and flaws.

We as people look for validation from our peers, and even from strangers, the people we don't even know.

Why is it important what other people think about us? When we spend so much time wondering what someone thinks of us, it gives us less time to embrace who we really are, because we begin to loose ourselves with the thoughts of others. Then we have to spend time finding ourselves.

Embrace yourself. Embrace your flaws.

What makes you perfectly imperfect?

_____

_____

_____

_____

_____

Dictionary.com. Computer software. Dictionary.com. Vers. 7.1.1. Dictionary.com LLC, 26 Jan. 2016. Web. 19 Oct. 2016. <Dictionary.com>.

The Holy Bible, new international version. (1984). Grand Rapids: Zondervan Publishing House.

There's Power In Your "I Am"
I AM. YOU ARE. PERFECTLY IMPERFECT LLC.

I Am Important

DEFINITION: IMPORTANT – To be of great significance.

*I*t begins with our thoughts of feeling important. We only feel what we think of ourselves.

Yes, there are people who may be in better situations financially, physically or even emotionally, but does that make that person better or more important than us? No it doesn't. You are here on this Earth individually designed for the purpose that God has for you. Everyone doesn't have the same skill or the ability that you have, and that's what makes you important.

What are you great at? What makes you stand out from the crowd? What is your gift?

In him we were also chosen, having been predestined according to the plan of him who works out everything in conformity with the purpose of his will, in order that we, who were the first to hope in Christ, might be for the praise of his glory. And you also were included in Christ when you heard the word of truth, the gospel of your salvation. Having believed, you were marked in him with a seal, the promised Holy Spirit, who is a deposit guaranteeing our inheritance until the redemption of those who are God's possession- to the praise of his glory. (Ephesians 1: 11-14)

Now, what makes you important?

_____

_____

_____

_____

_____

Dictionary.com. Computer software. Dictionary.com. Vers. 7.1.1. Dictionary.com LLC, 26 Jan. 2016. Web. 19 Oct. 2016. <Dictionary.com>.

The Holy Bible, new international version. (1984). Grand Rapids: Zondervan Publishing House.

THERE'S POWER IN YOUR "I AM"
I AM. YOU ARE. PERFECTLY IMPERFECT LLC.

I Am Equipped

DEFINITION: EQUIPPED – To be furnished with intellectual or emotional resources.

No one was put on this Earth without a purpose. Everyone has a career, a ministry or a vision they can excel in but may feel intimidated because of fear, lack of support, or by looking at how someone else who may be excelling a little more quickly. If there is something that you have a burning desire to accomplish, no one can take that away from you. Only if you don't allow them to. Be careful not to share your vision with everyone. There are people who you may share your vision with who may distract you from your vision with their negatives thoughts, opinions, and ideas. What you are equipped with is yours. Protect it.

2 Timothy 3:17

"So that the man of God may be thoroughly equipped for every good work."

Ephesians 2: 10

"For we are God's workmanship, created in Christ Jesus to do good works, which God prepared in advance for us to do."

What did God equip you to do?

_____

_____

_____

_____

_____

Dictionary.com. Computer software. Dictionary.com. Vers. 7.1.1. Dictionary.com LLC, 26 Jan. 2016. Web. 19 Oct. 2016. <Dictionary.com>.

The Holy Bible, new international version. (1984). Grand Rapids: Zondervan Publishing House.

THERE'S POWER IN YOUR "I AM"
I AM. YOU ARE. PERFECTLY IMPERFECT LLC.

I Am Valuable

DEFINITION: VALUABLE –Having qualities worthy of respect and admiration.

*Y*our value has nothing to do with your valuables. Jesus believes that we are so valuable that he took a chapter of the Bible to talk about it. In Luke chapter 15 he tells three stories about the lost son, the lost sheep, and the lost coin. Each story ends with the exact final phrase: Jesus says, "You matter!"

You are valuable. You matter to God. God says you are valuable because he loves you. He cares so much that he gave his life for you. He made only one you. You are unique. You are unlike anyone else who has ever lived. You may be feeling worthless, drained, or like you can't go any further. In your mind life has probably thrown more at you than you can handle but remember God says: "No temptation has overtaken you except what is common to mankind. And God is faithful; he will not let you be tempted beyond what you can bear. But when you are tempted, he will also provide a way out so that you can endure it" (1 Corinthians 10: 13).

What makes you valuable?

_____

_____

_____

_____

_____

Dictionary.com. Computer software. Dictionary.com. Vers. 7.1.1. Dictionary.com LLC, 26 Jan. 2016. Web. 19 Oct. 2016. <Dictionary.com>.

The Holy Bible, new international version. (1984). Grand Rapids: Zondervan Publishing House.

THERE'S POWER IN YOUR "I AM"
I AM. YOU ARE. PERFECTLY IMPERFECT LLC.

I Am Strong

DEFINITION: STRONG – Powerful in influence, authority, resources, or means of prevailing or succeeding.

As we go through life, we will cross many bumps in the road. But as we cross these bumps, we have to stand strong and believe that all of our help comes from God. There is always a story at the end of each season of our lives. This is why it is very important to surround yourself with those who will maximize your strength and not drain your strength.

Staying strong in God will renew your strength. Look toward the hills from which cometh our help.

Philippians 4:13
"I can do all things through Christ that strengthens me."

How are you strong?

_____

_____

_____

_____

_____

Dictionary.com. Computer software. Dictionary.com. Vers. 7.1.1. Dictionary.com LLC, 26 Jan. 2016. Web. 19 Oct. 2016. <Dictionary.com>.

The Holy Bible, new international version. (1984). Grand Rapids: Zondervan Publishing House.

THERE'S POWER IN YOUR "I AM"
I AM. YOU ARE. PERFECTLY IMPERFECT LLC.

I Am Capable

DEFINITION: CAPABLE –Having power and ability.

There comes a time in our life where we may feel defeated, confused, and even frustrated. It feels like we live in a house of destruction, where everything that comes our way triumphs over us. This destruction, which we call life's obstacles, will lead us into our victory. Because we are God's creation and we belong to him, he gives us victory through our Lord Jesus Christ.

God can handle any situation we give him. No problem is too tough for him. Nothing is beyond his ability. Believe in who you are and what you can do because you are capable.

Exodus 18:25
"He chose capable men from all Israel and made them leaders of the people, officials over thousands, hundreds, fifties and tens."

What are you Capable of?

_____

_____

_____

_____

_____

Dictionary.com. Computer software. Dictionary.com. Vers. 7.1.1. Dictionary.com LLC, 26 Jan. 2016. Web. 19 Oct. 2016. <Dictionary.com>.

The Holy Bible, new international version. (1984). Grand Rapids: Zondervan Publishing House.

THERE'S POWER IN YOUR "I AM"
I AM. YOU ARE. PERFECTLY IMPERFECT LLC.

I Am Enough

DEFINITION: ENOUGH – Adequate for the want or need.

D o you ever wake up feeling like you lost control of your life? You have no clue what you have been doing these last five, ten, or twenty years of your life. You're questioning everything you have done and have not done. You feel like you lost relationships or a job because of your actions. Despite all these things and everything else that may be going on in your life, you are good enough. Remember that life has its ups and downs and we are going to feel disappointments. The most important thing to remember is that you will never stay down for long—as long as you don't allow yourself to.

No one or anything should be able to disconnect you from who God has called you to be. Many of us feel like we have to earn our self-worth. You don't need another place, person, or thing to make you whole. God already did. You are enough!

Psalm 138: 8

"The Lord will fulfill his purpose for me; Your love, O Lord, endures forever – do not abandon the works of your hands."

I am enough because...

_____

_____

_____

_____

_____

Dictionary.com. Computer software. Dictionary.com. Vers. 7.1.1. Dictionary.com LLC, 26 Jan. 2016. Web. 19 Oct. 2016. <Dictionary.com>.

The Holy Bible, new international version. (1984). Grand Rapids: Zondervan Publishing House.

THERE'S POWER IN YOUR "I AM"
I AM. YOU ARE. PERFECTLY IMPERFECT LLC.

I Am My Thoughts

DEFINITION: THOUGHTS – The act or process of thinking.

Your happiness, health, success, and belief that you can overcome any obstacle and difficulty all depend on your thoughts. In order for positive thinking to be effective you need to adopt the attitude of positive thinking in everything you do. Use more positive words in your daily conversations. Visualize a better outcome in negative situations. Ignore what other people say or think about you. The power of your thoughts can shape or destroy the different situations that you may encounter. Take your power back—even when people are looking at you crazy. Remember, they are your thoughts, not theirs. The journey of your life depends on the quality of your thoughts. Changing the way you think and the way you look at things can lead you to an open road to drive towards your success and your happiness.

Psalm 13:2

"How long must I wrestle with my thoughts and day after day have sorrow in my heart? How long will my enemy triumph over me?"

What do you think of yourself?

_____

_____

_____

_____

_____

Dictionary.com. Computer software. Dictionary.com. Vers. 7.1.1. Dictionary.com LLC, 26 Jan. 2016. Web. 19 Oct. 2016. <Dictionary.com>.

The Holy Bible, new international version. (1984). Grand Rapids: Zondervan Publishing House.

THERE'S POWER IN YOUR "I AM"
I AM. YOU ARE. PERFECTLY IMPERFECT LLC.

I Am My Own Validation

DEFINITION:–VALIDATION- To give official approval to.

*I*s it healthy to want to feel validated? We would say yes. Ultimately, the most fulfilling form of validation comes from within. Life is a job on its own, and the more we look for something else external to validate us, the more we will be taken out of the present and be on the constant search for external validation.

Galatians 1: 10

"Am I now trying to win the approval of men, or of God? Or am I trying to please men? If I were still trying to please men, I would not be a servant of Christ."

How much do you judge yourself rather than value yourself? Recognize your feelings and consciously value them.

It's time to start loving yourself. What do you love about yourself?

_____

_____

_____

_____

_____

What will you not accept from yourself?

_____

_____

_____

_____

Dictionary.com. Computer software. Dictionary.com. Vers. 7.1.1. Dictionary.com LLC, 26 Jan. 2016. Web. 19 Oct. 2016. <Dictionary.com>.

The Holy Bible, new international version. (1984). Grand Rapids: Zondervan Publishing House.

THERE'S POWER IN YOUR "I AM"
I AM. YOU ARE. PERFECTLY IMPERFECT LLC.

I Am Not My Past But I Am My Future

DEFINITION: PAST – Gone by or elapsed in time.

FUTURE – Something that will exist or happen in time to come.

You are not your failed marriage.

You are not the child you once were.

You are not the bad things that happened to you.

You are not your suicidal attempts.

You are not the choices you've made.

You are not the rumors that was spread about you.

You are not your past.

Your future connects with your thoughts. Why not step out on faith and believe that God will never leave you nor forsake you? Your future is in a little box in God's hand. Go forth and get what's yours, for God said, "And I will do whatever you ask in my name, so that the Father may be glorified in the Son" (John 14:13).

Isaiah 55:11

"So shall my word be that goes out from my mouth; it shall not return to me empty, but it shall accomplish that which I purpose, and shall succeed in the thing for which I sent it."

It's time to let go of everything that tends to creep in your thoughts to bring you down. You are now your possibilities.

What do you need to leave in the past?

_____

_____

_____

_____

_____

Where do you see yourself in your future?

_____

_____

_____

_____

Dictionary.com. Computer software. Dictionary.com. Vers. 7.1.1. Dictionary.com LLC, 26 Jan. 2016. Web. 19 Oct. 2016. <Dictionary.com>.

The Holy Bible, new international version. (1984). Grand Rapids: Zondervan Publishing House.

THERE'S POWER IN YOUR "I AM"

I AM. YOU ARE. PERFECTLY IMPERFECT LLC.

I Am My Shift

DEFINITION: SHIFT – To transfer from one place, position or person.

*W*hat are you focused on? Are you focused on the job that you can't stand? Are you focused on what people are saying or thinking about you? Are you focused on the man or that woman that has left you? Are you focused on the abortion that you had? Are you focused on the crew that you used to hang with? If you focus on all of your personal wrongs, you increase your suffering and become angrier or even depressed.

What if you intentionally shift your thoughts to the desires of your heart? What would it feel like to give more energy or thought to what you want to accomplish in the next year? What could become of it?

Ecclesiastes 2:24

"There is a time for everything, and a season for every activity under heaven:

a time to be born and a time to die,

a time to plant and a time to uproot,

a time to kill and a time to heal,

a time to tear down and a time to build,

a time to weep and a time to laugh,

a time to mourn and a time to dance,

a time to scatter stones and a time to gather them,

a time to embrace and a time to refrain,

a time to search and a time to keep and a time to throw away,

a time to tear and a time to mend,

a time to be silent and a time to speak,

a time to love and a time to hate,

a time for war and a time for peace."

What is your next move personally and professionally?

_____

_____

_____

_____

Dictionary.com. Computer software. Dictionary.com. Vers. 7.1.1. Dictionary.com LLC, 26 Jan. 2016. Web. 19 Oct. 2016. <Dictionary.com>.

The Holy Bible, new international version. (1984). Grand Rapids: Zondervan Publishing House.

THERE'S POWER IN YOUR "I AM"

I AM. YOU ARE. PERFECTLY IMPERFECT LLC.

I Am Blessed

DEFINITION: BLESSED- Supremely favored.

*D*oes having a successful career, obedient children, a healthy body, a blissful marriage, financial abundance and trusted friends make you abundantly blessed? Than we wouldn't have to turn to God because we would feel self- sufficient, right? Everything would already be perfect and there would be no need to cry out to God. We would feel satisfied.

Remember earthly blessings are temporary. As easily as God has given them to us is as quickly as they can be taken away. Blessings are not defined as the material things that we have. We experience God's richest blessings in the most painful events. We become stronger in faith. We gain a deeper love and closer walk with God. The divorce, the bankruptcy, the loss of a job, death of a loved one, and every trial that you have gone through will ground your faith in ways that prosperity and abundance in material things can never do.

So many people are struggling. There are people that are worse off then you. The biggest blessing that you have overcome today was opening your eyes to see another day. Stop worrying about the material things that you don't have, but think about what God has blessed you with internally. You can hold your head up and say, "I don't have to worry because God is with me. I am blessed."

Matthew 5: 1-12

"Blessed are the poor in spirit, for theirs is the kingdom of heaven.

Blessed are those who mourn, for they will be comforted.

Blessed are the meek, for they will inherit the earth.

Blessed are those who hunger and thirst for righteousness, for they will be filled.

Blessed are the merciful, for they will be shown mercy.

Blessed are the pure in heart, for they will see God.

Blessed are the peacemakers, for they will be called sons of God.

Blesse are those who are persecuted because of righteousness, for there is the kingdom of heaven.

Blessed are you when people insult you, persecute you and falsely say all kinds of evil against you because of me. Rejoice and be glad, because great is your reward in heaven, for in the same way they persecuted the prophets who were before you."

Philippians 4:19

"And my God will supply all your needs according to his riches in glory in Christ Jesus."

There are some things that you want and you haven't received yet, but what are you blessed with at this very moment?

_____

_____

_____

_____

Dictionary.com. Computer software. Dictionary.com. Vers. 7.1.1. Dictionary.com LLC, 26 Jan. 2016. Web. 19 Oct. 2016. <Dictionary.com>.

The Holy Bible, new international version. (1984). Grand Rapids: Zondervan Publishing House.

THERE'S POWER IN YOUR "I AM"

I AM. YOU ARE. PERFECTLY IMPERFECT LLC.

I Am Incomparable

DEFINITION: INCOMPARABLE – Matchless and unequaled.

Your fingerprints, like your DNA, and your voice are so individual that no one in this entire universe can replicate you. No one has your exact gift, calling, or destiny. The Creator specifically assigned you uniquely for your life story. The biggest enemy that we struggle with as people is comparison. With the constant comparison of trying to be like what we see in society and social media, it strips us daily from our own special gift of being ourselves.

Some people have brown eyes or blue eyes, some people can do this, some people can do that, some people are right handed, some people are left handed. Each of us was made with a purpose. If you continue to walk through the light that God has illuminated for you, eventually it will shine more brightly.

An original is always greater than a copy.

Psalm 139: 13-14

"For you created my inmost being; You knit me together in my mother's womb. I praise you because I am fearfully and wonderfully made; Your works are wonderful, I know that full well."

What makes you stand out, incomparable?

_____

_____

_____

_____

_____

Dictionary.com. Computer software. Dictionary.com. Vers. 7.1.1. Dictionary.com LLC, 26 Jan. 2016.

Web. 19 Oct. 2016. <Dictionary.com>.

The Holy Bible, new international version. (1984). Grand Rapids: Zondervan Publishing House.

THERE'S POWER IN YOUR "I AM"
I AM. YOU ARE. PERFECTLY IMPERFECT LLC.

I Am Free

DEFINITION: FREE- Independent of my own will, thoughts, choice, and actions.

Being free is letting go of your obstacles:
- abusive relationship,
- suicidal thoughts,
- heartbreaks,
- substance abuse,
- sexual abuse,
- judgment,
- depression,
- negativity.

Your past hurt does not define you and has not become a part of your identity. It happened so that you could share how you have been delivered from what the Devil designed to destroy you. The one thing that the Devil forgot was that God has the final say-so. Letting go of heavy burdens releases streams of living water into our lives and enables God to do a new work in us. With the heavy weight of blocks that has been stacked on us, one of the greatest works of Christ brings us to a place in our life where we can forgive those who have hurt us.

Jesus says in Luke 11:2-4

"When you pray, say: Father, hallowed be your name, your kingdom come. Give us each day our daily bread. Forgive us our sins, for we also forgive everyone who sins against us."

Set your soul free, for this day forth God will reign in your life forever.

John 8:36

"So if the son sets you free, you will be free indeed."

There are many things that I AM free from, but today I free myself from...

_____

_____

_____

_____

_____

_____

Dictionary.com. Computer software. Dictionary.com. Vers. 7.1.1. Dictionary.com LLC, 26 Jan. 2016. Web. 19 Oct. 2016. <Dictionary.com>.

The Holy Bible, new international version. (1984). Grand Rapids: Zondervan Publishing House.

THERE'S POWER IN YOUR "I AM"

I AM. YOU ARE. PERFECTLY IMPERFECT LLC.

I Am My Own Peace

DEFINITION: PEACE – Freedom of the mind from any strife, annoyance, distraction, anxiety, and obsession.

We all encounter brutal experiences that unsurprisingly knock us down and off course for a period of time. We feel that money is essential for us to enjoy life, but the pursuit of money causes immense problems and anxiety. Even our friends and family can also bring us a lot of worry and heartache.

Our mental calmness depends highly on our ability to calm our thoughts. Instead of focusing on the past, focus on the present moment that you are living in now. It's already better, so hold your head up. Our journey isn't supposed to be easy; it's supposed to be worth it.

John 14: 27

"Peace I leave with you; my peace I give you. I do not give to you as the world gives. Do not let your hearts be troubled and do not be afraid."

Today I release my peace by freeing my mind from the thoughts of...

_____

_____

_____

_____

_____

Dictionary.com. Computer software. Dictionary.com. Vers. 7.1.1. Dictionary.com LLC, 26 Jan. 2016. Web. 19 Oct. 2016. <Dictionary.com>.

The Holy Bible, new international version. (1984). Grand Rapids: Zondervan Publishing House.

THERE'S POWER IN YOUR "I AM"
I AM. YOU ARE. PERFECTLY IMPERFECT LLC.

I Am Qualified

DEFINITION: QUALIFIED – Provided with proper and necessary knowledge and skills.

*W*hen we look over our lives, we have overcome so many obstacles that tried to hold us back. We begin to reflect and think, "How in the world did I get from point A to point C?" When you trust in the name of the Lord, he will see you through. You may not think you are qualified, but God will make your credentials sufficient in any eye.

2 Corinthians 3:5

"Not that we are sufficient in ourselves to claim anything as coming from us, but our sufficiency is from God."

What are you qualified to do?

_____

_____

Dictionary.com. Computer software. Dictionary.com. Vers. 7.1.1. Dictionary.com LLC, 26 Jan. 2016. Web. 19 Oct. 2016. <Dictionary.com>.

The Holy Bible, new international version. (1984). Grand Rapids: Zondervan Publishing House.

THERE'S POWER IN YOUR "I AM"
I AM. YOU ARE. PERFECTLY IMPERFECT LLC.

I Am Passionate

DEFINITION: PASSIONATE – Expressing, showing, or marked by intense or strong feeling.

Passion gives us a drive, but more than that, it makes us feel that we have a purpose in our lives. Being passionate can be very difficult at times. It's not about knowing but also feeling that you are on the right path. Ask God to speak his words of assurance and to guide you in the right direction.

Colossians 3:23

"And what so ever ye do, do it heartily, as to the Lord, and not unto men."

What are you strongly passionate about?

_____

_____

Dictionary.com. Computer software. Dictionary.com. Vers. 7.1.1. Dictionary.com LLC, 26 Jan. 2016. Web. 19 Oct. 2016. <Dictionary.com>.

The Holy Bible, new international version. (1984). Grand Rapids: Zondervan Publishing House.

THERE'S POWER IN YOUR "I AM"
I AM. YOU ARE. PERFECTLY IMPERFECT LLC.

I Am Transparent

DEFINITION: TRANSPARENT – Open, frank, candid.

Transparency is one of the greatest gifts that we have received and also the greatest gift that we love to give. It allows others to see in, which enables us to see out. Transparency allows people to see and hear what you have overcome. It's showing people how you have been delivered from heartache, a broken heart, homeliness, addiction, etc. It's being truthful and real with everyone.

Does being transparent mean that you are telling all of your business? No, we don't think so. We believe that it is supporting someone who may be sitting right next to you and may be going through the very same thing that you have been delivered from. Just from your story, you have helped someone.

Hebrews 13: 16

"And do not forget to do good and to share with others, for with such sacrifices God is pleased."

What if your story could help someone else who may be going through the same thing that you have conquered? Wouldn't you think your story is worth telling?

What is your story?

_____

_____

_____

_____

_____

_____

Dictionary.com. Computer software. Dictionary.com. Vers. 7.1.1. Dictionary.com LLC, 26 Jan. 2016.Web. 19 Oct. 2016. <Dictionary.com>.

The Holy Bible, new international version. (1984). Grand Rapids: Zondervan Publishing House.

THERE'S POWER IN YOUR "I AM"
I AM. YOU ARE. PERFECTLY IMPERFECT LLC.

I Am Focused

DEFINITION: FOCUSED – To concentrate on a central point or idea.

*T*here will be plenty of distractions that will come your way and take you away from the path you are supposed to be on.

The only reason why goals would stop working is because the person who has set the goals chose to give up on them.

Tips on staying focused:
- Concentrate on one to three goals.
- Create a vision board.
- Create milestones.
- Create a plan.
- Document your goals progress.

Matthew 6:33

"But seek ye the first kingdom of God, and his righteousness, and all these things shall be added unto you."

Name one thing that you are focusing on, whether it is professionally or personally. Now state the first step that you will take to get closer to your goal.

_____

_____

_____

_____

_____

_____

_____

Dictionary.com. Computer software. Dictionary.com. Vers. 7.1.1. Dictionary.com LLC, 26 Jan. 2016. Web. 19 Oct. 2016. <Dictionary.com>.

The Holy Bible, new international version. (1984). Grand Rapids: Zondervan Publishing House.

THERE'S POWER IN YOUR "I AM"
I AM. YOU ARE. PERFECTLY IMPERFECT LLC.

I Am Confident

DEFINITION: CONFIDENT – Sure of oneself; having no uncertainty about one's own abilities, correctness, and successfulness.

*Y*ou want to be in a relationship or married again but fear that you would do something to mess it up. You want to start a business but fear that it is too difficult to do. You want to start a new job but are afraid to leave your current job because you feel that your job is your source. You want to be a writer but fear it is too difficult to get published and therefore your story is stagnant in your notebook. You want to begin something new but are afraid and unsure of yourself and your confidence to move forward.

It's time to tap into the confidence that you were born with and silence the threats of the thoughts of fear. Don't weigh your confidence on what you can do and what you know, but base it on what you are willing to learn along the way.

Philippians 4: 13

"I can do everything through him who gives me strength."

Do you believe in yourself? Are you afraid of what you may not become?

What are you ready to successfully become?

_____

_____

_____

_____

_____

_____

Dictionary.com. Computer software. Dictionary.com. Vers. 7.1.1. Dictionary.com LLC, 26 Jan. 2016. Web. 19 Oct. 2016. <Dictionary.com>.

The Holy Bible, new international version. (1984). Grand Rapids: Zondervan Publishing House.

THERE'S POWER IN YOUR "I AM"

I AM. YOU ARE. PERFECTLY IMPERFECT LLC.

I Am Not Defeated

DEFINITION: DEFEATED — To eliminate or deprive of something expected.

L ife right now might feel hard. When we are dealing with struggles in our lives they are not created to defeat us, but to make us stronger. Feeling defeated is only temporary. It's when we give up that makes it endless.

2 Corinthians 4: 8-10

"We are hard pressed on every side, but not crushed; perplexed, but not in despair; Persecuted, but not abandoned; struck down, but not destroyed. We always carry around in our body the death of Jesus, so that the life of Jesus may also be revealed in our body."

What in your life at this point has you feeling defeated (e.g. cancer, divorce, loss of a job, loneliness, un-forgiveness, rejection, death)? Have you given it the permission to take over your thoughts and emotional being?

Are you ready to reclaim your thoughts?

Write down what you thought defeated you and leave it here.

_____

_____

_____

_____

_____

_____

Dictionary.com. Computer software. Dictionary.com. Vers. 7.1.1. Dictionary.com LLC, 26 Jan. 2016. Web. 19 Oct. 2016. <Dictionary.com>.

The Holy Bible, new international version. (1984). Grand Rapids: Zondervan Publishing House.

THERE'S POWER IN YOUR "I AM"
I AM. YOU ARE. PERFECTLY IMPERFECT LLC.

I Am Successful

DEFINITON: SUCCESSFUL – Having attained wealth, position, honors, or the like.

*I*t doesn't matter what you do for a living, how old you are, or where you are from. We all want to be successful. Everyone's definition of being successful may be different. Some people define success as being wealthy, having power, or having fame. Some people equate success with being a faithful wife or husband or a responsible parent. We all just want to achieve success so that we can live comfortable lives. In order to get to this point, you have to think outside of the box. Think big. Figure out what you love to do and do it. Do not be afraid of the word "No" because it only means that there is something greater for you. Believe in your capacity to succeed and be willing to work hard.

Deuteronomy 8: 18

"But remember the Lord your God, for it is he who gives you the ability to produce wealth, and so confirms his covenant, which he swore to your forefathers, as it is today."

What are you planning on being successful in? Write your vision and make it plain...

_____

_____

_____

_____

_____

_____

Dictionary.com. Computer software. Dictionary.com. Vers. 7.1.1. Dictionary.com LLC, 26 Jan. 2016. Web. 19 Oct. 2016. <Dictionary.com>.

The Holy Bible, new international version. (1984). Grand Rapids: Zondervan Publishing House.

THERE'S POWER IN YOUR "I AM"
I AM. YOU ARE. PERFECTLY IMPERFECT LLC.

I Am Not My Mistake

DEFINITION: MISTAKE — An error in action, calculation, opinion, or judgment caused by poor reasoning, carelessness, or insufficient knowledge.

*I*t's time to acknowledge your mistake and then let it go. You are not alone. Everyone makes mistakes and it is sometimes hard to let them go and forgive yourself, but did you ever think that it was all a part of the plan for your life?

(1) Except the mistake.

(2) Reflect on the mistake.

(3) Now grow from the mistake.

Now it's time to finally release the mistake!

1 Peter 5: 6-7

"Humble yourselves, therefore, under God's mighty hand, that he may lift you up in due time. Cast all you anxiety on him because he cares for you."

Write it here and leave it here. It's time to move forward. Your future is waiting for you!

_____

_____

_____

_____

_____

_____

Dictionary.com. Computer software. Dictionary.com. Vers. 7.1.1. Dictionary.com LLC, 26 Jan. 2016. Web. 19 Oct. 2016. <Dictionary.com>.

The Holy Bible, new international version. (1984). Grand Rapids: Zondervan Publishing House.

THERE'S POWER IN YOUR "I AM"
I AM. YOU ARE. PERFECTLY IMPERFECT LLC.

I Am Not My Struggle

DEFINITION: STRUGGLE – To contend with an adversary or opposing force.

On this quest that we call life, we hit so many hurdles whether financially, emotionally, physically, professionally, or personally. We give the struggle so much power that it begins to overshadow the testimony that is supposed to come from the test. Shouldn't we just say yes to the struggle and go through the struggle? Some may say that it is easier said than done. And yes we agree. There are some struggles that individuals go through that we would not be able to handle, but look at how that makes you special! Your test and your struggle was built just for you! God knows who he can trust with his assignment.

1 Peter 5: 10

"And the God of all grace, who called you to his eternal glory in Christ, after you have suffered a little while, will himself restore you and make you strong, firm and steadfast."

What are you struggling with? Write it down and come back and reflect on it once you have surpassed it! Watch how you have won at the end of it all!

_____

_____

_____

_____

_____

_____

Dictionary.com. Computer software. Dictionary.com. Vers. 7.1.1. Dictionary.com LLC, 26 Jan. 2016. Web. 19 Oct. 2016. <Dictionary.com>.

The Holy Bible, new international version. (1984). Grand Rapids: Zondervan Publishing House.

THERE'S POWER IN YOUR "I AM"
I AM. YOU ARE. PERFECTLY IMPERFECT LLC.

I Am More Than A Conqueror

DEFINITION: CONQUEROR – To be victorious; to gain, win, obtain by effort or personal appeal.

$\mathcal{I}$n life there are trials and tribulations that come our way. We sometimes feel like they are here to literally just shut us down. There are some who will walk away from their trials and ones who will fight their trials, verbally, physically, and/or violently. Has there ever come a time in your life where you grew tired of the same things happening over and over again?

When do you began to seek God's face? When do you begin to desire God's heart? If we seek God in the beginning of every tribulation, how will things be different? God has done great things over and over again, and he declares that we are victorious over our adversaries.

Romans 8: 37-39

"No, in all these things we are more than conquerors through him who loved us. For I am convinced that neither death nor life, neither angels nor demons, neither the present nor the future, nor any powers, neither height nor depth, nor anything else in all creation, will be able to separate us from the love of God that is in Christ Jesus our Lord."

What are you ready to conquer? Write it down and work towards it. It starts with a pen: "Faith without works is dead" (James 2:14-26 KJV).

_____

_____

_____

_____

_____

Dictionary.com. Computer software. Dictionary.com. Vers. 7.1.1. Dictionary.com LLC, 26 Jan. 2016. Web. 19 Oct. 2016. <Dictionary.com>.

The Holy Bible, new international version. (1984). Grand Rapids: Zondervan Publishing House.

The Holy Bible, King James Version. New York: American Bible Society: 1999; Bartleby.com, 2000. www.bartleby.com/108/.

THERE'S POWER IN YOUR "I AM"

I AM. YOU ARE. PERFECTLY IMPERFECT LLC.

I Am Not The Generational Curse

DEFINITION: GENERATIONAL — A group of individuals belonging to a specific category. In this case your parents/grandparents.

CURSE — The cause of evil, misfortune, or trouble.

*g*enerational curses are spiritual bondages that are passed down from one generation to another, and a continual negative pattern of something being handed down from generation to generation.

Our Story:

Our mother, Mrs. Deloris Rogers-Watkins aka "Dee," was married and divorced; my twin sister and I both were married as well and now are both divorced. Wow! As we write this, it's still shocking how life works. Our mother is now happily married and daily my sister and I speak that we will both be happily married someday! People have heard our stories and would immediately say, "Twins, both of you are divorced? It must be something wrong with you two." Well, to answer the question that you may have now: Are we perfect? No. Did we love our spouses? Sure did. Were they the ones created for us? Nope, but we wish them nothing but happiness.

Ezekiel 18:20

"The soul who sins is the one who will die. The son will not share the guilt of the father, nor will the father share the guilt of the son. The righteousness of the righteous man will be credited to him, and the wickedness of the wicked will be charged against him."

It's time to break that generational curse today, so speak this: "Curse, there is no room for you in my destiny, so I'm going to write you down right here and leave you here to stay."

Dictionary.com. Computer software. Dictionary.com. Vers. 7.1.1. Dictionary.com LLC, 26 Jan. 2016. Web. 19 Oct. 2016. <Dictionary.com>.

The Holy Bible, new international version. (1984). Grand Rapids: Zondervan Publishing House.

THERE'S POWER IN YOUR "I AM"

I AM. YOU ARE. PERFECTLY IMPERFECT LLC.

I Am Not This Disease

DEFINITION: DISEASE – An illness that affects a person; a condition that prevents the body or mind from working normally.

*D*o you ever ask yourself the question, "why me?" Try to turn your question around and ask yourself, "why *not* me?" God never puts more on us than we can bear, but the question is, how can you use what you are going through to help someone else? Start by speaking healing to your own body. Stop waiting for someone else to pray for you and lay hands on yourself. All it takes is faith the size of a mustard seed and the three simple words, "I am healed!"

Psalm 103: 2-5

"Praise the Lord, O my soul, and forget not all his benefits who forgives all your sins and heals all your diseases, who redeems your life from the pit and crowns you with love and compassion, who satisfies your desires with good things so that your youth is renewed like the eagles."

Jeremiah 17:7

"Heal me, O Lord, and I will be healed; save me and I will be saved for you are the one I praise."

Speak your healing today. I am healed from...

_____

_____

_____

_____

_____

_____

Dictionary.com. Computer software. Dictionary.com. Vers. 7.1.1. Dictionary.com LLC, 26 Jan. 2016. Web. 19 Oct. 2016. <Dictionary.com>.

The Holy Bible, new international version. (1984). Grand Rapids: Zondervan Publishing House.

THERE'S POWER IN YOUR "I AM"
I AM. YOU ARE. PERFECTLY IMPERFECT LLC.

I Am Not My Misfortune

DEFINITION: MISFORTUNE – An instance of mischance, mishap; bad luck.

There are times in our lives where we run into disappointments, anxiety, catastrophes, or just bad news. We get to the point where we just want to give up. We want to isolate ourselves from the world. We want to throw in the towel. We get so comfortable and content when everything is going well in our lives that we become complacent with where we are. As soon as a misfortune happens, it pushes us into an uncomfortable position.

What if this discomfort was the breakthrough to your next level? What if this misfortunate has to take place to push you to be greater? Would you be willing to go through this process? Would you be able to stand up to this adversity and say, "Is that all you have?"

Don't look at the misfortune as negative, but as the steps that God is taking you through to make you stronger and wiser. He's calling you to win not fail!

Genesis 41:52

"The second son he named Ephraim and said, "It is because God has made me fruitful in the land of my suffering."

Lay your misfortune right here and speak the outcome that you wish to see. You can speak from where you are right now!

This misfortune no longer has a hold on me...

_____

_____

_____

_____

_____

Dictionary.com. Computer software. Dictionary.com. Vers. 7.1.1. Dictionary.com LLC, 26 Jan. 2016. Web. 19 Oct. 2016. <Dictionary.com>.

The Holy Bible, new international version. (1984). Grand Rapids: Zondervan Publishing House.

THERE'S POWER IN YOUR "I AM"
I AM. YOU ARE. PERFECTLY IMPERFECT LLC.

I Am My Promise

DEFINITION: PROMISE – An express assurance on which expectation is to be based; Indication of future excellence and achievement.

We are all accustomed to promises. We are also accustomed to broken promises. People break promises daily. Sometimes circumstances are beyond our control, but what about the promise to yourself and the promise made by God? A promise is of no more value than the ability of the one who makes it to carry through. So why not gain your own control of your promise and put in back in the hands of God—the one who promises to supply every need we have?

What organization do you want to start? What is the title of the book that you want to write? What does your clothing line look like? What are your burning desires?

Mark 11:24

"Therefore I tell you, whatever you ask for in prayer, believe that you have received it, and it will be yours."

What are you trusting God for? God has given you the vision, but it is up to you to execute it. What is your promise? How are you going to execute it?

_____

_____

_____

_____

_____

Dictionary.com. Computer software. Dictionary.com. Vers. 7.1.1. Dictionary.com LLC, 26 Jan. 2016. Web. 19 Oct. 2016. <Dictionary.com>.

The Holy Bible, new international version. (1984). Grand Rapids: Zondervan Publishing House.

THERE'S POWER IN YOUR "I AM"
I AM. YOU ARE. PERFECTLY IMPERFECT LLC.

I Am Restored

DEFINITION: RESTORED – To be Renewed, Refreshed, Revived.

*H*ave you gotten to the point in your life where you feel like you need a fresh start from the situations that you may be going through or have gone through? When we willingly allow the Holy Spirit to begin the process of restoration in our lives, then he will place a new season with a new revelation and new life. The Holy Spirit is the restorative agent here on Earth. Once we surrender to him, then he will restore everything in our lives that needs to be restored.

Joel 2: 25-26

"I will repay you for the years the locusts have eaten, the great locusts and the young locust, the other locust and the locust swarm –my great army that I sent among you. You will have plenty to eat until you are full, and you will praise the name of the Lord your God who has worked wonders for you; never again will my people be shamed."

Today is the day restoration can begin!

Write down what you want restored in your life, and begin to speak, "I am restored." It begins by acknowledging your restoration in order to revive your state of health and soundness.

_____

_____

_____

_____

_____

Dictionary.com. Computer software. Dictionary.com. Vers. 7.1.1. Dictionary.com LLC, 26 Jan. 2016. Web. 19 Oct. 2016. <Dictionary.com>.

The Holy Bible, new international version. (1984). Grand Rapids: Zondervan Publishing House.

THERE'S POWER IN YOUR "I AM"
I AM. YOU ARE. PERFECTLY IMPERFECT LLC.

I Am A Survivor

DEFINITION: SURVIVOR – One who continues to function or prosper in spite of opposition, hardship, or setbacks.

*M*aybe you lost your job, have been diagnosed with an illness, have had several miscarriages or lost a loved one. Maybe someone walked out on you. Despite the feeling of discouragement and what you've been through, know that things are going to get better.

Deuteronomy 31:5

"The Lord himself goes before you and will be with you; he will never leave you nor forsake you. Do not be afraid; do not be discouraged."

Things are already looking better! Survival begins with a spoken word. What have you survived? Even when you can't see it, believe it and write it here…

_____

_____

_____

_____

_____

_____

Dictionary.com. Computer software. Dictionary.com. Vers. 7.1.1. Dictionary.com LLC, 26 Jan. 2016. Web. 19 Oct. 2016. <Dictionary.com>.

The Holy Bible, new international version. (1984). Grand Rapids: Zondervan Publishing House.

THERE'S POWER IN YOUR "I AM"
I AM. YOU ARE. PERFECTLY IMPERFECT LLC.

I Am Worth It

DEFINITION: WORTH – Usefulness or importance to a person, or for a purpose.

*Y*ou might feel that every rejection that you have received over this past year has devalued your self-esteem to make you feel less than the next person. Delayed does not mean denial.

We as humans wonder why someone who may not work as hard as you could have it so easy. We have to realize that what they go through and what they accomplish is their story that was created just for them. Just look at how important you are. You are worth being the author of your own story because only you can tell it. You are an author, and you didn't even realize it!

Psalm 139: 13-14

"For you created my inmost being; You knit me together in my mother's womb. I praise you because I am fearfully and wonderfully made; Your works are wonderful, I know that full well."

Look at how important you are to our God! He has entrusted in you to share with his people the gift that he has given you. God has something greater for you, but you have to stop comparing yourself to the next person.

What makes you worth it?

_____

_____

_____

_____

_____

_____

Dictionary.com. Computer software. Dictionary.com. Vers. 7.1.1. Dictionary.com LLC, 26 Jan. 2016. Web. 19 Oct. 2016. <Dictionary.com>.

The Holy Bible, new international version. (1984). Grand Rapids: Zondervan Publishing House.

THERE'S POWER IN YOUR "I AM"
I AM. YOU ARE. PERFECTLY IMPERFECT LLC.

I Am My Vision

DEFINITION: VISION – The act or power of anticipating that which will or may come to be: prophetic vision.

*H*as there ever been a time in your life where all types of ideas and thoughts and moves that you want to make continue to pop into your head? You have thoughts to start a clothing line, open up a car wash, write a book, or start some type of business. You consistently have a burning desire in your heart to do something. Did you ever think that this is the assignment sent to you? This may be one of your life's purposes?

God gives us so many visions. He knows us better then we know ourselves, but it is up to us and it is our job to reveal the vision that God has given us. It will never happen if we continue to sit on the vision that God had given us.

Habakkuk 2:2

"Write down the revelation and make it plain on the tablets so that a herald may run with it."

What vision did God place in your thoughts? How are you going to step out in your vision?

_____

_____

_____

_____

_____

Dictionary.com. Computer software. Dictionary.com. Vers. 7.1.1. Dictionary.com LLC, 26 Jan. 2016. Web. 19 Oct. 2016. <Dictionary.com>.

The Holy Bible, new international version. (1984). Grand Rapids: Zondervan Publishing House.

THERE'S POWER IN YOUR "I AM"
I AM. YOU ARE. PERFECTLY IMPERFECT LLC.

I Am In Control

DEFINITION: CONTROL – The act of dominating or commanding.

*D*o you ever feel like you just don't have control over your own life? You don't know if you are going left or right, forward or backwards. It's time to take your control back. You control who you are, where you will be, and what you will become. Take the control back over your life from whatever you have given the power to, whether it's from a person, a substance, depression, suicidal thoughts or any spirit who has you in an indecisive place.

Are you ready to take control over your life again? It starts with you. Declare today that you will be repossessing control back over your life.

Romans 8: 28

"And we know that in all things God works for the good of those who love him, who have been called according to his purpose."

This is not the end of you. Write down who or what may think they have control over your life and leave it here...

_____

_____

_____

_____

_____

_____

Dictionary.com. Computer software. Dictionary.com. Vers. 7.1.1. Dictionary.com LLC, 26 Jan. 2016. Web. 19 Oct. 2016. <Dictionary.com>.

The Holy Bible, new international version. (1984). Grand Rapids: Zondervan Publishing House.

THERE'S POWER IN YOUR "I AM"
I AM. YOU ARE. PERFECTLY IMPERFECT LLC.

I Am Consistent

DEFINITION: CONSISTENT – Agreeing or accordant; compatible; not self-contradictory.

*C*onsistency is a start to a new beginning in your life. Once you've made up in your mind that you will live and not die, it is imperative that you surround yourself with the covering of the Word and people that will keep you on the path to the vision that God has for you. Yes, because you have decided today that you are ready to make a difference in your life, distractions are about to come for you left and right. But this is why it is so important that you protect yourself from environments, people, and things that will drain you and try to deter you from what God has for you. Right now write down every distraction that is in your life that can hinder you from making it to your serendipity. It's okay to distance yourself from people who may interfere with you making it to your destiny because some people and some situations are only in your life for a season and you have some that will be there for a lifetime.

So starting today, get a head start on weeding out the ones who will not fit into your divine purpose.

Ecclesiastes 9: 10

"Whatever your hand finds to do, do it with all your might, for in the grave, where you are going, there is neither working nor planning nor knowledge nor wisdom."

Let's start your list today. Who will no longer fit on the ride to your destiny?

_____

_____

_____

_____

_____

_____

Dictionary.com. Computer software. Dictionary.com. Vers. 7.1.1. Dictionary.com LLC, 26 Jan. 2016. Web. 19 Oct. 2016. <Dictionary.com>.

The Holy Bible, new international version. (1984). Grand Rapids: Zondervan Publishing House.

THERE'S POWER IN YOUR "I AM"

I AM. YOU ARE. PERFECTLY IMPERFECT LLC.

I Am Me

DEFINITION: ME – The objective case of "I".

Do you think that there is anyone that can go through what you are going through or what you have gone through? We both have reflected on each other's situations that we have gone through in this thirty-three years of life, and both have stated to each other, "That could not have been me." We are identical twin sisters born sixty seconds apart, but we each had to go through our own tests and trials to reach the vision that God had given us so that we could write this book. We never had any thoughts of becoming authors, but what we realized was God had given us the power to speak to our pain, and with that we began to have peace. We began to have joy. We began to live again. Because of his power, we know that we can accomplish and think beyond our own imaginations. Because we take the limits off of our God and ourselves, even when it seems dark, the light gets so much brighter at the end of the tunnel.

James 4: 6
"Humble yourselves before the Lord, and he will lift you up."

Confess who you are and what you will become.
I AM ...

_____

_____

_____

_____

_____

_____

Dictionary.com. Computer software. Dictionary.com. Vers. 7.1.1. Dictionary.com LLC, 26 Jan. 2016.,Web. 19 Oct. 2016. <Dictionary.com>.

The Holy Bible, new international version. (1984). Grand Rapids: Zondervan Publishing House.

THERE'S POWER IN YOUR "I AM"
I AM. YOU ARE. PERFECTLY IMPERFECT LLC.

Jerimiah 29:11 (KJV)

"FOR I KNOW THE PLANS I HAVE FOR YOU, "DECLARES THE LORD, PLANS TO PROSPER YOU AND NOT TO HARM YOU, PLANS TO GIVE YOU HOPE AND A FUTURE."

The Holy Bible, King James Version. New York: American Bible Society: 1999; Bartleby.com, 2000. www.bartleby.com/108/.

THERE'S POWER IN YOUR "I AM"
I AM. YOU ARE. PERFECTLY IMPERFECT LLC.

I am healed.

I am delivered.

I am a survivor of suicidal attempts.

I am loved.

I am courageous.

I am a woman of faith.

I am important.

I am wise.

I am unique.

I am powerful.

I am stronger.

I am beautiful.

I am confident.

I am fearless.

I am immovable.

I am determined.

I am happy.

I am more than what you see.

I am as my Creator made me.

I am enough.

I am blessed.

I am Deloris Rogers's twin girl #2.

I am perfectly imperfect.

I am Kerese Millen.

THERE'S POWER IN YOUR "I AM"

I AM. YOU ARE. PERFECTLY IMPERFECT LLC.

I am my story.

I am God's child.

I am healed from my divorce.

I am a woman of faith.

I am a conqueror.

I am not the lies told on me.

I am love.

I am grateful.

I am a fighter.

I am a survivor of generational curses.

I am alive.

I am free.

I am a survivor of depression.

I am not my mistakes.

I am at peace.

I am happy.

I am worth fighting for.

I am a winner.

I am Deloris Rogers's twin girl #1.

I am perfectly imperfect.
I am Kristle Millen

THERE'S POWER IN YOUR "I AM"
I AM. YOU ARE. PERFECTLY IMPERFECT LLC.

The Beginning Of A New You

SPEAK YOUR "I AM"

Right now at this very moment, how would you describe your "I AM"?

"I AM...

_____

_____

_____

_____

_____

_____

Reflections

_____

_____

_____

_____

_____

_____

_____

_____

_____

_____

_____

_____

_____

_____

_____

_____

_____

_____

_____

_____

_____

_____

_____

_____

_____

THERE'S POWER IN YOUR "I AM"
I AM. YOU ARE. PERFECTLY IMPERFECT LLC.

Acknowledgements

𝓕irst and foremost we will like to thank You, our Heavenly Father, for entrusting in us to share the gift of help across the world. You have and continue to trust us with the path that you have specifically assigned to us, and we say thank you. You love us so much that you taught us the power of "I AM" through our own life stories. Thank you, Daddy, for being our resource, our provider, our hero, our healer, our comfort in the midst of loneliness, our strong tower and our protector. Thank you for being a Majestic God!

To Deloris: our Mommy, our role model, our prayer partner, our rock, our biggest supporter. We could not have prayed for a more immeasurable, incredible, fascinating, classy and the most giving, praying, God seeking mother. Your unconditional love and support throughout our journies has helped make this rocky ride a little smoother, and for that we thank you.

To John Millen Jr., our Dad. We love you and thank you for your love and support.

To our family and friends who have played a role in our lives, we don't take any of you for granted and we love you to life.

To our COO Danielle Townsend and CMO Akhia Palmer of I AM. YOU ARE. PERFECTLY IMPERFECT LLC: You two have rocked with us from the birth of our organization and we are so grateful for the one hundred percent dedication to the vision that God has given us. Your hard work does not go unnoticed. We love you two.

To The I AM. YOU ARE. PERFECTLY IMPERFECT LLC. Team: Tania Davis, Amanda Jones,

LaToya Knighten Douglas, Kai Douglas, Sharita Taylor, Tammy Adams, Deanka Hart, Regina Stallworth and Nieshah Dismukes: Words cannot express the gratitude of the hard work, love, and support that you have demonstrated throughout our events and charities. We love you girls to the moon and back.

To our pastor and first lady John and Anna Hannah, we thank you for being obedient in saying "Yes" to God's will and speaking the word that God gives you weekly. New Life Covenant Southeast is a weekly lifesaver.

To our brother William A. Eaddy, II: From the first day that we met you, you have prayed, encouraged, and pushed us to continue and to not give up even when we were in doubt. We love you and thank you for being the brother that we always wanted.

To Lauran Smith and Kenneth Daley: You two have been there since our first event, "Kreate A Kloset," hosting and keeping the crowd laughing. We thank you for your sincere prayers and support. We genuinely love you both.

We would personally like to thank Ikeysha Clincy for your referral with the publishing and editing company. You definitely took a weight off of our shoulders. We love you. We would like to thank our makeup artist and little sister Nicole Richardson. She is the owner of Flawless Beauty. Thank you for always making time for us, even when it's last minute. We love you. If you need an amazing makeup artist who travels the world, contact Nicole at www.flawlessbeautybynicole.com.

To one of the best photographers in this entire world, Tania Davis Photography: Words can't express how you have highlighted our vision in so many different pictures. We are so ever grateful for your consistent professionalism and love. If you are in the Chicago area and need a photographer contact Tania Davis Photography at www.taniadavisphotography.com.

I, Kerese, would like to thank my son Princeton who is now six years old. Wow how time flies. I love you beyond words. I pray that your "I Am" takes you to the destiny that only God has assigned for you.

I, Kristle, would like to thank my new smile, my backbone, my early morning encouragement, my laugh, my protector, my heart, my love, my future: Mel Estes. You continue to demonstrate the role of a man that covers and seals a relationship, and I'm so grateful for what God has in store for the two of us!

THERE'S POWER IN YOUR "I AM"

I AM. YOU ARE. PERFECTLY IMPERFECT LLC.

KERESE & KRISTLE MILLEN

About The Authors

Kristle holds a master's degree in Early Childhood Education from Northern Illinois University, with a Type 04 certification, a Special Needs Endorsement and a Post Doctorate Certificate of Advance Studies in Curriculum and Instruction with an Endorsement in English as a Second Language.

Kerese holds a master's degree in Teaching, Learning and Assessments, with her bachelors in Early Childhood Education.

Kerese also has her Post Doctorate Certificate of Advance Studies in Curriculum and Instruction with an ESL endorsement.

Kerese and Kristle are both teachers, motivational speakers, authors, mentors and CEOs of I Am. You Are. Perfectly Imperfect LLC, which comprises an inspirational blogging website (that can be found at www.iamyouareper-fectlyimperfect.com), an inspirational clothing line, and events that inspire and empower one to change their way of thinking.

Kerese and Kristle currently work with children and families for the city of Chicago as educators to the children of their communities and as mentors and supervisors to up-and coming future teachers.

Kerese and Kristle have a vision of a world where people learn to respect, accept, and embrace the differences as the core of what makes life so fascinating.

Kerese and Kristle both born, raised and reside in Chicago, Illinois.

THERE'S POWER IN YOUR "I AM"

I AM. YOU ARE. PERFECTLY IMPERFECT LLC.

Connect with Kerese and Kristle Millen on Social Media:

Facebook page: Kristle Kerese Millen

Facebook business page: I Am. You Are. Perfectly Imperfect LLC

Instagram business page: @iamyouareperfectlyimperfect

@millentwin1

@millentwin2

Email: Iamyouareperfectlyimperfect2@gmail.com

If you would like to keep up with upcoming events and purchase I Am. You Are. Perfectly Imperfect apparel, please visit www.iamyouareperfectlyimperfect.com and click on the appropriate links.

CPSIA information can be obtained
at www.ICGtesting.com
Printed in the USA
FSOW03n0140070217
30490FS